How to Grow
Your Soul

Amaya Pryce

Cover and Interior Design:
John H. Matthews, bookconnectors.com

Original cover art by Tina Tarnoff (etsy.com)

Dedicated to the Wellness Institute in Issaquah, Washington – with loving gratitude for my Wolf Pack

TABLE OF CONTENTS

INTRODUCTION
Ego and Soul

I go around doing nothing but persuading both young and old not to care for your body or your wealth in preference to your soul.
~ Socrates

In a very real sense the title of this book is misleading: You can never actually "grow" your soul, because it is already whole, complete and perfect. But you *can* grow your connection to and understanding of soul, and it isn't even hard to do. Your soul wants to be known and expressed. I see it as more of an opening process, as if all of the potential of your Authentic Self is held within a seed that only requires a bit of sun and water to crack open and begin to expand. All it takes from you is a willingness to allow the process of opening.

Although you may not be aware of it, in every moment, in every thought you think and action you take – from the most boringly trivial to the earth shattering – you are making a decision. Think of it as casting a vote of sorts: In each separate moment of your life you have the choice to identify yourself with either your ego or your soul. If life were a reality show (irony intended), we'd have Team Ego and Team Soul. Allow me to introduce you.

Ego is that tall guy over there – the one with all the looks, money and status. On the surface he's the easy winner, and he has the legions of adoring fans to prove it. He's bulging with muscle and oozing confidence, the guy that women want to be with and men want to be. A head-turner, for sure.

Soul is a bit harder to spot. He's a quiet guy, easily overlooked in all the hype and commotion that follow Ego around (and he likes it that way). In spite of this, there's a quiet strength and power that radiate from Soul. He doesn't seem to do much, but things always get done when he's in charge. And people feel good around him. With Ego, they never seem to measure up.

Soul has a way of bringing out the best in everyone around him.

Many people – most – overlook Soul and put their money on Ego. It looks like a smart bet, and everyone else is doing it. Often it seems to work out just fine, at least in the beginning. Ego *does* win a lot. (He tends to be somewhat ruthless and driven, which definitely helps.) But eventually, many of his supporters become disillusioned. The wins are showy, but Ego doesn't really give a lot away. In fact, as time goes by he expects more and more from his followers, while giving less and less in return.

Not that Ego's a bad guy. In fact, he sincerely believes that he's doing you a favor. The problem is, he's completely self-absorbed, and so it's literally all about him. What's good for him *must* be good for you, right? Hmm. Soul's followers, on the other hand, seem to gain in satisfaction and happiness as time goes by. There's a quiet strength and power about them, too. Nothing flashy, nothing obvious, but they can change a room or a situation simply with their presence. On Team Soul, the wins might come a little later, but the pay-off is huge.

So which one sounds like the best bet to you now? Which one gets your vote? It's easy to jump on Ego's bandwagon: Everything looks so bright and shiny and everyone seems to be having such a good time. Almost everyone in your life will pat you on the back when you go for Ego, too. There are some powerful reinforcers for this choice: praise, money, power and influence, to name a few. Just feeling part of the "in" crowd. It can be hard to pass up that immediate, temporary gratification and assurance for the long-term, lasting rewards of Soul.

But in the end Ego is a house of cards, a hall of mirrors. It's all about appearances, with very little substance. Scratch just a little beneath the slick exterior and you'll find fear, Ego's prime motivator. When you depend on Ego, your house is built on the proverbial sand, rather than a strong foundation of rock. The moment something comes along to disturb the balance, everything falls apart. The mirage evaporates – poof! – and there you are, alone on the bandwagon with a bunch of old confetti. Ego is not a good companion when the chips are down. For that, Soul's your man.

The wise choice seems clear when we talk about ego and soul like this, but it's not as obvious when we're caught up in day-to-day life. Much of society and our past programming incline us toward ego. There's a lot of weight and momentum pushing us along that path, and it will take intention and awareness just to slow down the momentum long enough to realize that there *is* a choice to be made. Then the challenge is to make your choice mindfully, moment by moment, rather than simply casting an absentee ballot.

In this book we'll take a look at the choices you have in some specific areas of life – relationships, work and play – and how to use them to wean yourself off your attachment to ego and deliberately grow your connection to soul. We'll also look carefully at the thorny issue of difficulties and dark times: What happens when life isn't going the way your ego wants it to go, and how these can be the very times that grow your soul the most.

This is nothing less than the path of enlightenment, which to me means being 100% identified with the soul and 100% *dis*-identified with the ego. "Letting go of your ego" doesn't mean becoming some sort of robot or otherworldly saint, without likes and dislikes, social roles and responsibilities, or your own distinctive personality. It simply means that you don't identify your sense of self and well-being with them. You're not attached to them. You operate from the soul's agenda (which is love, connection and inner growth) rather than the ego's (fear, separation and material success). There's no need to see ego as an enemy to overcome. It's more like a well-meaning, but misguided, servant that's been put in a position of power it's not equipped to handle. Ego's only a problem when we let it call the shots.

Likewise, growing your soul isn't an arduous process that requires you to give up things you find pleasurable or to always put other people first. This is not an invitation to add more struggle to your life! Actually, if you've read my previous book, *5 Simple Practices for a Lifetime of Joy,* you'll know that I'm all about making things as simple and effortless as possible. The truth is, nothing is more stressful and less fun than constantly trying to meet the demands of your ego, or to get the world to live up to your ego's expectations. Once you've experienced the ease and joy of living from the soul, you'll never want to go back, I promise.

In this book, as in my last one, I'll be quoting and referring to many of my favorite writers and teachers, with a list of suggested reading included at the end. There is truly nothing new under the sun, and I like it that way. As the French writer André Gide put it, "Everything that needs to be said has already been said. But, since no one was listening, everything must be said again."

Although the same truths have been taught for millennia, my hope is that hearing them one more time, with a slightly different spin, will prove to be the charm for you. Personally, I find that these truths sink in deeper with each repetition. It's much easier to know and agree with something intellectually than it is to put it into practice consistently. I should know! But I fervently believe that life will conspire with you to give you exactly the experiences and information you need, once you make a commitment to the soul's agenda of love and personal growth.

It's an exciting journey that begins with a simple decision – a declaration of allegiance, as it were. And all it takes from you, in any one moment, is simply to cast your vote, not for the ego, but for the soul.

I treasure my soul as something given into my keeping, something that I must keep intact – more, keep in a state of growth and awareness whatever the odds.
~ May Sarton

Run my dear from anyone or anything that does not strengthen your precious budding wings.
~ Hafiz

CHAPTER ONE
The Power of Choice

Moment by moment our practice is like a choice, a fork in the road: we can go this way, we can go that way. It's always a choice, moment by moment...

~ Charlotte Joko Beck

In my first book I wrote about the power of *attention* to change your life, but there's a crucial step that comes before attention: Choice. What you put your attention on grows, that's true. But first you have to decide where to put your attention. And how, in this complex, changing, fast-moving world, do we know where to put our attention?

Sometimes it feels like all we can do is constantly react. From the moment we open our eyes in the morning (probably in reaction to an alarm going off), to the first imperatives of the day (getting dressed and fed and out the door, or getting someone else dressed and fed and out the door, or both), to the social and news media that bombard us all, and so on throughout the day until we collapse in bed at night, most of us career like pinballs from one bumper to another, not so much choosing where to put our attention as letting it be chosen for us.

This is momentum in action. It feels inevitable because we're so familiar with it and because everyone else seems to be on exactly the same roller coaster with us. But it's not inevitable; it's a *choice*. This gets tricky here, because many of the circumstances in your life may very well not be under your direct control (at least not immediately). I get that.

The beauty of this path – the path of soul growth – is that the choice doesn't depend at all on your outer circumstances. You don't have to abandon your family or your job and move to a cave in the Himalayas to achieve soul growth. Good thing, because that would count the vast majority of us out.

The initial choice that we need to make is an internal one, not external. In time, that internal choice will lead to plenty of external changes, but you don't need to start there. In fact, one of my central beliefs about life is that *there are no mistakes.* In other words, where you are is exactly where you need to be for your optimal good.

Now again, that doesn't mean that you should necessarily *stay* in any situation, particularly an unsafe one, just because you find yourself there. It may have been the perfect growth mechanism to get you where you are today... and not one second longer. But, aside from those truly toxic situations (and you know who you are), any circumstances at all can serve as the perfect incubator for your growth.

The perfect vehicle

One of my favorite teachers and mentors, the life coach and writer Dr. Martha Beck, once said that no one need question whether they're on the path to reach enlightenment. If you're alive, she said, "You've already bought the ticket." We'll all get there one day, at the perfect time, no matter how far off course we seem to have come. That's a comforting thought.

Taking the metaphor a step further, I like to think that whatever circumstance is in front of you, in this moment, is the *perfect vehicle* for this stretch of the road. You might have a rickshaw or a broken-down bicycle right now, but if that's what's in front of you, you can trust that it's absolutely perfect for your path right now. And it will change.

You might have a Lamborghini (metaphorically)… and that will change too. It's not really about the vehicle, but about the path, the journey. It's easy to look at other people's circumstances and wish we were on their paths, but sitting down by the side of the road and wishing for a different vehicle will literally get you nowhere. Better to take up the vehicle you have – even if it's just your own two feet – and set off down the road, knowing that where you are is exactly where you're supposed to be.

Choosing to embrace your present circumstances is the necessary first step to changing them. You'll never reach that next perfect vehicle waiting for you if don't step forward to meet it. The life you have now, the challenges you have now, the relationships, the work, the living situation: All are perfect grist for the mill. We can use all of them on this quest for growth.

There's a pervasive myth floating about that we somehow need an ideal, pristine environment in order to be "spiritual." When the kids are out of the house, when we have enough money to go on that retreat, when we retire... *then* we'll have time to think about our souls. The irony is that paying attention to and growing your connection to soul makes all the other challenges much easier to handle. As the classic saying puts it: "You should sit in meditation twenty minutes a day, unless you're too busy. In that case, you should sit for an hour."

The point is, now is the only time we have. Spiritual writer and teacher A.H. Almaas says: "Only now is real. And it is always like that. At each moment, only that moment exists. So we need to ask why we put ourselves on hold, waiting for the right time, waiting for the right circumstances to arise in the future. Maybe the right time will never come. Maybe the conditions you have in mind will never come together for you. When will you begin to exist then? When will you begin to be here, to live?"

Yes, making a sea change like this can feel overwhelming. Can you really do things differently, or will you just get sucked right back into the old habits of mind and behavior? After all, we're talking about turning around an ocean liner that's been cruising full-speed in one direction for quite a while. And yet, even that change of course can be accomplished with just a small metal rudder, and time.

The shift in focus that you make, from ego to soul, is like that rudder. At first the change may seem imperceptible. Certainly it requires time and repetition. Remember, the choice isn't made just once, but over and over again, moment by moment. Every moment you have a new chance to focus: Will it be ego or soul? Fear or love? Unconsciously or not, you are always choosing. The real shift is to be *aware* of the choice, and then to make it consciously. What will you choose in this moment?

The three levels of self

To make an intelligent choice in any sphere of life you have to understand your options. "Ego" and "soul" are both words that carry a lot of baggage, so it would probably be a good idea to unpack them before we go any further. One way to visualize them is to consider the difference between your Social Self and your Authentic Self, as shown in the figure below:

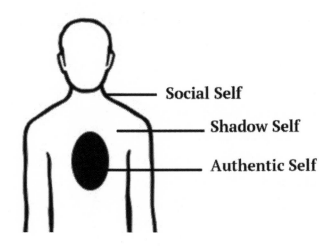

Social Self

Shadow Self

Authentic Self

The **Social Self**, or ego, is the self that we present to the world, the part that most people *think* is who they really are. We often use the term "ego" in a relative way (as in "he has such a big ego") but here we're using it in a broader sense, to include all of the roles, social masks, habits and personal preferences that we accrue gradually, over time, as we interact with the world. This definition of ego doesn't automatically imply arrogance or a high sense of self-esteem. True self-esteem comes from knowing and being at home with who you *really* are, at the core of your being.

Your Social Self, in contrast, is a temporary, changeable persona that is completely *other-*

referenced, which means that we develop it in reference to how we want others to see us, and what we want the outer world to provide for us (security, love, money, sex, and so on). We begin to construct this self at a very young age, in response to rewards and punishments – intended or not – that are doled out by our primary caregivers and others.

Ego is the sum of all the layers of (mostly subconscious) pretense and defense that we use to gain what we think we need from the world and protect us from losing what we have. Its primary motivator is fear, and its benign intent is to keep us safe. Unfortunately, being ultimately unreal, ego *always* involves illusion and self-deception.

The **Authentic Self**, or soul, is completely independent of this ego structure. In the diagram it's pictured as an island at the center of your being, but in reality it has no physical location or limits. The Authentic Self is who you *really* are, the part of you that isn't born and doesn't die, the part that's both delightfully personal and unique and, at the same time, completely un-separate and un-separateable from everything else in the Universe.

You didn't create your Authentic Self, and it doesn't change in relation to circumstances and others' reactions. It's completely *self-referenced,* which is not the same as being selfish (more on that below). Unlike the Social Self, which was created over time and can be intentionally modified, the Authentic Self is eternal and perfect, just waiting to be revealed and expressed. This is who you are at the core of your core, and it's the source of true and lasting joy, peace and fulfillment in life.

To complicate things just a bit, there's a third layer of selfhood we need to understand: The **Shadow Self**. This is who we're *afraid* we really are, all the scary, sad, angry, wild and unacceptable bits we want to keep hidden from the world (and even ourselves). Picture it as a stormy sea just under the surface of the Social Self, held tightly in check by defenses we put in place to keep it out of sight and under control. Unfortunately, the only way to discover the bliss of the Authentic Self is to dive into this shadow sea and swim across it – but most people put one foot in that water and immediately head back to the familiar safety of the shore. Then they build up their ego defenses even higher to avoid the possibility of slipping back in.

The task we face in growing our souls is to take a deep breath, dive into the things that scare us (the very things ego wants to protect us from), and keep on swimming. Fortunately, there are life rafts that will help keep your head above water as you swim: books, teachers, therapists, wise friends, and many practices like meditation, prayer and journaling. You will become a stronger and more confident swimmer as you gain practice, and soon you'll begin to feel the magical pull of your soul, calling you home.

The journey home to your Authentic Self is what this book is about. There may be a sense of safety and familiarity in ego, but there isn't much joy. And, ironically, the safety of being at home in your soul is a thousand times more comforting than the brittle armor of the Social Self. Once you find this place of unconditional love and joy, you'll never want to leave it.

Self-referenced vs. other-referenced

And that place – the Authentic Self, or soul – is where we're heading in the following chapters, starting with relationships. Relationships are the perfect place to start, because by definition they tend to be other-referenced, just like the Social Self. We develop our egos in response to others, almost from the first moment we arrive in these Earth-suits.

Very small children are delightfully self-referenced. They don't care about (or even have a concept of) what they might look like to anyone else. They don't spend a lot of time or energy worrying about whether they're a success in the eyes of the world. They are just who they are, period. Animals have this same wonderful egoless-ness: Can you imagine a cat or dog giving a damn about whether his coat is brown or black or multi-colored? As the poet David Whyte wrote: "All the birds and creatures of the world are unutterably themselves..."

Which brings up an important point: Ego does not equal *personality*. And choosing soul over ego doesn't mean you automatically become a spineless blob, without wants and needs. On the contrary. Both animals and small children have plenty of personality, experience strong emotions, and have instinctive needs for food, shelter and socialization. As long as they're warm and comfortable and safe and fed and not bored, they're usually pretty good with life. But they'll let you know if they're not… until they're taught otherwise.

Pretty early on we humans (and even very socialized animals) get the message that some of our emotions and needs and wants aren't as okay as others, and we begin the process of splitting ourselves in two, polishing up the presentable side and hiding all the rest – the Shadow Self – under the rug.

Many people think that to be a "good" person you must be selfless. A good person puts other people and their needs first, doesn't feel sad or angry or scared, never makes a scene. Most of us buy this myth wholesale. Please don't. This is just another (more covert) way of being other-referenced, but it's every bit as manipulative as someone who pursues the ego's agenda more directly. It's easy to recognize an egotist climbing ruthlessly up the corporate ladder, and a bit shocking to throw your long-suffering mother in the same class, but both may in fact be operating from the Social Self, albeit on opposite ends of the spectrum.

This gives you some sense of how confusing, or at least unfamiliar, it can be to navigate the soul/ego divide. You'll need to throw out a lot of your most cherished assumptions and learn to keep returning to what your "gut" tells you is true *for you*. That's the only compass that will always give you true north, and most of us have no idea how to use it. We'll keep practicing as we walk through the various parts of your life. If you're like me, you've spent so much time steering by the wrong star (ego) that it will take some time to re-calibrate your inner guidance system to the soul and learn to trust its input.

To use another metaphor, the world has been blaring out a loud and catchy tune all your life that everyone else seems to be dancing to. Your challenge is to train your ear to tune in to the "still, small voice" of your Authentic Self that's been broadcasting all the time under that external cacophony. It can be done, but probably not overnight. And when you stop dancing, people will notice and *not* approve.

Following your soul can feel a bit lonely at first. You might lose a few friends, and maybe even some important relationships. Some of those people might call you selfish when you begin to change, so be prepared for that.

Martha Beck calls this the "empty elevator" syndrome, and it can be pretty unnerving. Gradually your elevator will fill back up with people who really get you, who love your Authentic Self and not just the spiffed up Social Self, but the time alone in the elevator is scary and you'll be tempted to run back to the cozy companionship of the ego crowd.

I've experienced the empty elevator syndrome myself, and watched it up close as my daughter went through high school. Was there ever a sturdier bastion of ego than high school? I doubt it. It's where many of us learned our most poignant lessons about fitting in (or not). We learned to let other people tell us what we want, what to think, and how to behave to get ahead in the world. For many of us, this is when the Social Self really took over and we learned to abandon ourselves – our Authentic Selves – while merging into the collective "other."

The good news is that your Authentic Self has not abandoned *you*. It's still there, waiting patiently for you to wake up from your long identification with the Social Self. Certain attitudes and practices will be especially helpful to you in the process of awakening. Think of them as "force multipliers" that can be used in any situation or circumstance to help you let go of illusion and realign with soul.

Force multipliers

In military-speak, a force multiplier is any additional factor (outside of the actual forces involved) that contributes to the likelihood of a mission's success. One of the most important allies you can take along on your journey of awakening is an attitude of **curiosity**. Just get interested and start noticing. I guarantee that you'll be surprised at what you find. The first thing you'll probably notice is that certain situations and people make you feel *off*. Maybe you can't put a finger on why, but you know that you just can't be yourself in those situations. You're not comfortable, you don't feel at home, you hardly even recognize yourself. Perfect! This is exactly what we're looking for.

At first it will probably take fairly blatant examples to get your attention, but with practice you'll get very good at noticing when that feeling comes up, even if it's very subtle. It's like waking up your "bull-s**t meter," although it's yourself that you're calling out, whenever you find that you're faking it in social settings or buying into the ego's illusions in some other form. With curiosity, you don't need to invite along any judgment. Just show it the door whenever it turns up, because judgment is *not* a force multiplier. It's ego again.

Another important ally to deliberately harness is the force of your **intention.** I do this by writing out and frequently repeating to myself statements about what I'm trying to achieve. These sound a lot like the old practice of writing affirmations, except that they're about how I want to show up in the world, not how much money I have in the bank. I change them frequently as new wording or new shades of meaning occur to me, and try to repeat them several times a day. Here are two I'm working with currently:

I choose to embody my soul fully and let go of ego and illusion to the greatest extent possible.

I choose to see everyone and everything through the eyes of Spirit.

That gives you an idea, but your own intentions will be unique to you and will evolve as you do. Ask yourself questions like: Why am I here? What do I want? How can I serve? I'm a huge believer in the power of intention as the foundation for all positive change. I think it sets in motion all kinds of helpful forces in the universe. Remember, your soul *wants* to be expressed in the world – it's what we came here for. But the gift of free will means that you will never be forced to give up your illusions. The intention and the willingness have to come from you.

Your final force multiplier is the most important but misunderstood practice of all: **Meditation.** I'm not asking you to go all Hare Krishna on me. You don't need to buy a zafu (even if you know what that is) or become a contortionist to meditate. The core of the practice is simply taking time, even a few moments, to intentionally stop the presses and step outside your normal whirlwind of activity (or the whirlwind of thoughts that normally take up your attention).

This can be accomplished by formally sitting down and watching your breath for twenty minutes, or by pausing to really *see* a flower or a bird or the sunset, to taste a cup of tea or listen to a beautiful piece of music. Here, too, intention is the key. If your intention is to temporarily disengage from ego and tune in to soul, it really doesn't matter much what form that takes. Your soul will hear the call and respond.

What makes meditation such a powerful force multiplier? The most important reason is that it gently coaxes you out of your mind (in a manner of speaking). The mind is where the Social Self rules supreme. While meditation doesn't actually stop your thoughts – that's mostly a myth – it does get you into the habit of stepping back from them so that you can notice that they're really just a story you're telling yourself.

Meditation helps to loosen the hold ego has on us and opens a direct line of communication with the soul. With practice it brings a treasure trove of wonderful gifts: clarity, peace of mind, presence, awareness, joy, wisdom. All that from stopping for a few minutes on a regular basis to turn inward. It's a bargain, believe me.

Choose you

The point of all these practices, the point of this journey we're about to take through your life, is to bring you home to your Authentic Self. All the good stuff is there. It's where you're meant to be. We spend so much energy, so many years of our lives creating what we think is an acceptable version of ourselves to present to the world, and then desperately shoring it up when it inevitably starts to crumble. It's exhausting and never-ending, and it distances us from a real experience of the world and authentic relationships with other people.

Psychotherapist and author John Welwood writes: "The pain that our [false] identity causes us arises from our larger intelligence – from our deeper being, which is suffering because we are not living as fully as we could. This more wakeful part of us feels the pain and constriction of being caught in a set of stories and beliefs, scripts and behaviors that cut us off from a rich and expansive openness to life. The nature of our being is an unconditional openness. We are born that way – curious, awake, and completely responsive to our environment – and unless we live that way, we will suffer."

Living from that deeper nature is simply a choice, made in the present moment, over and over. It's not a mysterious process. It doesn't require supernatural powers. It's not even particularly difficult, especially in comparison to the alternative. In the following chapters we'll look at how that choice plays out in some specific situations – relationships, work, play, and the unavoidable dark times that visit every life.

The choice is always yours to make. So please, choose to be who you *really* are. You'll never look back.

It takes Courage to grow up and turn out to be who you really are.
~ e.e.cummings

Find out who you are, and then do it on purpose.
~ Dolly Parton

The chief happiness of a man is to be what he is.
~ Erasmus

CHAPTER TWO
Relationships

The meeting of two personalities is like the contact of two chemical substances: if there is any reaction, both are transformed.
~ *Carl Jung*

Relationships are the most effective catalysts for personal growth that I know. Although it's certainly possible – and often feels much easier – to grow your soul in splendid isolation, there's no better place to road test those new insights than in relationship. Other people, from your spouse to your mom to the checker in the grocery store, are the sandpaper life kindly provides to smooth out your rough spots. Irritating, yes, but also indispensible for growth.

If you've ever attended a spiritual retreat, or spent a relaxing day alone in a beautiful setting that nurtures your spirit, you've probably experienced the letdown that occurs when you re-enter everyday life and discover that the kids' squabbling still makes you want to tear your hair out. It's amazing how quickly that Zen-like calm seems to disappear in "real life."

It would be great if those peak experiences would simply change us once and for all, but that rarely happens. What does happen is that we open up a little bit more, and then we're immediately given the opportunity to try to remain open under less ideal circumstances. If you see it as a game more than a test it won't frustrate you nearly as much! Even though it might feel like it, you'll never close back down completely. Every time you expand, you give your soul a little more room to manoeuver.

Soul growth definitely feels like it goes "two steps forward/one step back" much of the time. In fact, when you start down this path it often seems like your life gets *worse* for a while, but that's only because you become so much more aware of your feelings and reactions. As you learn to deliberately step out of your familiar numbing and coping mechanisms, everything can feel a bit raw. Just be patient with yourself and bring that attitude of curiosity into play.

And it also helps to remind yourself of this one essential truth: *There's no one else out there.*

Wait… what?

There's no one else out there

Okay, this is a strange one, but it's helped me a lot, so bear with me while I explain. Whenever something or someone bothers or upsets you, it's because they're triggering an unresolved wound or issue in *you*. This is good! It means we can stop looking outside ourselves for the solutions to our problems and upsets, and look inside instead. On the soul level, what happens "out there" isn't really the issue so much as what it triggers within us. The events and people in our lives are reflections of our own inner processes.

But wait a minute! People do some really crummy things! We can't just let them off the hook for their behavior, can we? That would just make us doormats!

Good point. Being "triggered" refers to the emotions you feel, not necessarily to the actions you take. The truth is, understanding your own triggers actually gives you far more power to take effective action in any situation than reacting unconsciously to a stimulus does. Often, much of our personal power is dissipated in emotions like anger, outrage, resentment and so on. Rather than addressing the problem calmly and effectively, we get caught up in the story we tell ourselves about it and the emotions that story triggers.

Those emotions are clues that, with some patient unraveling, can lead you back to earlier situations – usually in childhood – that evoked similar feelings in you. We all have certain basic themes that run through our lives, repeating themselves in various forms until we recognize and deal with them on a deeper level. If something keeps happening in your life, if some emotion (worry, fear, anger, envy, whatever) is practically automatic, that's not just coincidence, bad luck, or "the way things are."

Maybe we unconsciously recreate the same situations over and over, or maybe we just interpret every different situation through the same old lens, but the results are depressingly familiar. In *The Road Less Traveled,* M. Scott Peck writes, "Problems do not go away. They must be worked through or else they remain, forever a barrier to the growth and development of spirit." I would go further and say that working through these problems actually *constitutes* the growth and development of spirit.

Fixing what's out there never works for long, because the real problem is always "in here." Learning to identify your own patterns is a quantum leap in maturity level. Just being willing to take a peek inside first when something triggers you is a huge step that goes against every instinct we have.

Our animal instincts tell us to protect ourselves from irritation or threat through some manipulation of the other individual or situation: Attack or withdrawal. For animals, the reaction will usually be obvious and physical, but humans have the ability to play out the whole drama on an *internal* level as well. How many fights have you silently carried on with the people around you? How often have you withdrawn emotionally (if not bodily) as a manipulative or protective tactic?

This is the ego level of reaction, because ego always wants to protect itself, first and foremost.

Ego will always tell you that the problem is out there and that you are completely justified in being upset, in attacking or withdrawing. According to the ego, it's the other person or situation that has to change in order for you to feel okay.

Unfortunately, this belief will always keep you trapped. People might change for a while in response to your pleas or demands or manipulations, but in reality you're just plugging the dyke with a finger. We've all experienced that horrible *Groundhog Day* feeling of being caught in the same wretched story over and over. The only way you can permanently be free from the drama is to change yourself. But how exactly do you do that?

Start with curiosity and intention. The determination to understand and change will take you far. Keep reminding yourself: *There's no one else out there.* When you feel upset, see it as a red flag that something inside needs your attention. Certainly, take any actions that need to be taken on the outer level, but be very reluctant to assign blame or make the other person responsible for your upset. Your emotions belong to *you*, and that's ultimately a much saner way to live.

What I found, after spending a good while investigating my own reactions, is that my patterns started to present themselves to me as choices rather than inevitabilities. I would be in a situation that would ordinarily cause me to react in a certain way, but this time *I could see it* and actually make a choice about whether or not to go down that familiar path. Because I was aware of my own issues, I knew that what was really causing my distress wasn't the situation itself, but what it represented for me.

Here's an example: I was at a workshop, it was lunchtime, and I sat down at one of the available empty tables (I was one of the first through the buffet line, because I'm always hungry!). As other people started to file in, they sat in laughing, happy groups at all the other tables. Gulp. I started to get a familiar feeling. *I'm all alone. No one likes me. This is embarrassing. They all must be mean and shallow. Or maybe I'm just a loser.* Yada yada.

This time, however, a different voice broke into my inner dialogue. *Hey, look! This is your pattern! This is just that same feeling you had in elementary school. Wow, that's kind of interesting, how you immediately go there. Actually, it's kind of nice to have a little quiet time at lunch, and this food is really good. Maybe you should just relax and enjoy it.* Which is what I did, I'm happy to say.

Several other times during that same workshop I had similar experiences of watching myself start to get upset, recognizing how I would usually react (along with all the familiar justifications) and then choosing not to take that path. It was incredibly liberating! I wasn't at the mercy of my old programming or of anyone else's actions. I could see lots more options for myself once I stopped being upset. For instance, at lunch I could have simply moved over to join another group, an option I would never have seen or taken if I had gone with my old "they're all just mean" story.

Once I got on a roll, it actually became fun to watch my ego trying to spin everything as an attack or threat or even just an unreasonable inconvenience. I discovered that my ego has a pretty extensive list of demands and conditions it needs the world to meet in order for it to feel happy and safe. My soul is a whole lot more adaptable and relaxed, and much more fun to hang out with!

Since then I've become faster at recognizing when I'm getting triggered, so that sometimes it only takes seconds for a whole storyline to rise up in front of my eyes and be dismissed. Of course, that depends on the depth of the original wound and how much healing I've done in that area. Some of these original wounds are wide and deep, requiring multiple go-arounds to gradually heal from the inside out. These are the major life themes that often lead to our darkest moments, which we'll be looking at in Chapter Five.

Another unfortunate truth is that it's much easier to spot patterns in other people than it is in ourselves: That's called a blind spot. Blind spots are why we spend decades re-running the same old scripts, continually auditioning new people for the same roles. Bad boyfriend. Demanding boss. Unreliable friend. We also cast ourselves in familiar roles, and one of the most common is the role of Victim.

In fact, there's a whole scenario called the Victim Triangle that plays itself out over and over again in offices, living rooms, huts and palaces around the world. It's so pervasive that it deserves a section of its own, so come along with me to Co-Dependency World. We'll have plenty of company there.

Escaping the Victim Triangle

In the book *Breaking Free from the Victim Trap: Reclaiming Your Personal Power,* writer and therapist Diane Zimberoff illustrates the roles of Victim, Persecutor and Rescuer – roles we have all played at one time or another. The Victim Triangle, first described by Dr. Stephen Karpman in the 1960's, is the foundation of all co-dependent relationships. Co-dependency is far more prevalent than most people realize, and it very often has nothing to do with substance abuse. What it does have to do with is controlling anxiety. Each of the three roles is a characteristic pattern people use to control their own anxiety, and these patterns are played out in many a so-called "normal" relationship.

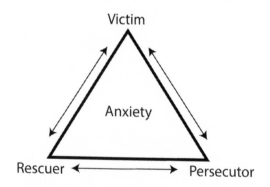

Although we all have one role that feels most comfortable, it surprised me to learn that we often switch roles quite readily, even in the midst of a single conversation. For example, I am most comfortable in the role of **Rescuer**. Now that I understand the dynamics involved, I see how that role reduces my anxiety: I get to feel powerful and good and needed, and I also get to control other people's behavior, often with their blessing. This feeling of control and power is a heady illusion for someone like me, who grew up trying to manage a somewhat rudderless home life. The rescuer role can feel like the "good guy" of the three but, if you're tempted to congratulate yourself for being one, realize that part of the payoff for rescuers is this very sense of virtue. Because rescuing is socially sanctioned, it may actually be the hardest of the roles to recognize and free yourself from.

The payoff for **Victims,** on the other hand, is to manage their anxiety by enlisting someone like me to rescue them from their sad fate, which of course is never their own fault. For them, handing over the reins means that not only are they not responsible for making any decisions, but there's always someone else to blame if the results aren't what they want. And the results are almost never what they want, because victims rely on an endless series of problems and circumstances to justify their feelings of helplessness and resentment.

(It's important to note here that all of these roles refer to psychological orientations. You can be the actual victim of a crime or abuse without necessarily taking on the victim role. You enter the Victim Triangle when you *identify* with the role and carry that identity forward into the rest of your life, beyond the original insult. The intent of this discussion isn't to minimize the real effects of victimization, but to differentiate them from the "victim mentality" that cedes personal responsibility in favor of blaming others. We all fall into this one on a regular basis, until we learn not to.)

As the final corner of the triangle, **Persecutors** control their anxiety more overtly through anger and dominance. On the surface, this one may seem like the easiest role to spot (and it's certainly the number one candidate for the position of "bad guy"), but if you dig a little deeper you'll find that most persecutors started out as victims, and still often identify with that role. And the deep-seated tendency most of us have to look for a bad guy – someone to blame – in any situation is a good indication that we're operating unconsciously within the Victim Triangle ourselves.

Are you beginning to get a sense of how complex and fluid these dynamics are? Rescuers can very easily morph into persecutors, and victims will often turn on their would-be rescuers and become persecutors themselves. You can play one role in some relationships and a different role in others, or multiple roles in the same relationship. The anxiety and lack of power underlying all three roles can lead to seething resentment. It's a three-ring circus, and the only way out is to recognize what's going on and step out of the dynamic. The Victim Triangle requires at least two players to function, so if you don't play, the whole game falls apart.

Let me give you an example of how it worked in my life before I became aware of what was going on. Many years ago we decided to adopt an older boy with a history of psychological problems. This is a laudable decision, and I went into it with the best of motivations, but unfortunately my tendency to play the rescuer set me up for several years of drama.

Our new son was an expert at playing the victim role, which I'm sure is why I attracted him into my life in the first place. (People who are adept at playing the Victim Triangle game tend to find each other easily.) Unfortunately, he resisted my rescuing attempts, and quickly slipped into the persecutor role in our family, with his wild behavior and acting out. I obligingly shifted to the victim role, feeling like my life was out of control, and when things got really bad I'd become a persecutor in turn, yelling at or punishing him, at which point he would immediately slip back into being a victim.

Can you see how anxiety fueled every step in this dance? I even ended up in the hospital a couple of times during this period with mysterious illnesses, which isn't typical for me. This might seem like an extreme example (okay, it was Crazytown), but if you look with open eyes you'll most likely see variations of this cycle occurring everywhere. Newspapers and magazines are full of them. Around and around she goes, and where she stops…

The only way to stop is to recognize that everything comes back to your own doorstep (because there's no one else out there). Once you become aware of the dynamic and your own characteristic pattern for dealing with anxiety, the game loses its power over you. No one can *make* you be a victim, or a persecutor, or a rescuer. You always have a choice. Always. Ego will tell you every time that other people or the situation are to blame, which feels good for a while, but keeps you endlessly stuck in the Victim Triangle. Soul takes responsibility (for your own actions, not for anyone else's) and gives you back the freedom to choose your reactions rather than playing an endless part by rote.

In my case, once I stepped out of the game, the perfect solution unfolded for all of us in the form of another adoptive family with the skill and resources to really help this boy. This is a good example of how following the soul's guidance can sometimes look "selfish" and bring down condemnation from the ego crowd, who are all too ready to make judgments and assign blame. Disrupting our adoption was a difficult and humbling step to take, but it has proven to be a blessing for everyone involved.

Shame, judgment and separation are common to both the ego and the Victim Triangle (and it's always the ego that gets you into the Victim Triangle in the first place). Neither one can function without an "other." You can't be a victim if there are no persecutors, and vice versa. They have to maintain their roles in order for you to have an identity, so it can be extremely threatening if one side refuses to play their part. But when you shift your focus enough to see that everyone around you is a reflection of yourself, there's no longer any point in dividing the world into right and wrong, enemies and friends, victims and persecutors.

Buddhist teacher Sharon Salzburg wrote, "There is no reason for a feeling of separation from anything or anyone, because we have been it all and done it all. How then can we feel self-righteous or removed from anyone or any action? ... Everyone we meet we know. Everything that is done we are capable of."

One challenging exercise that brings this home is to look at someone when they're doing something you're tempted to judge and think, "That's *me* when I'm stressed out." (Or running late or feeling insecure or whatever else seems appropriate to the situation.) Have you really never done something similar, or been tempted to? For example, my experience with our adopted son led me to a great feeling of compassion and sorrow for child abusers that I never could have imagined before. I can truly say with humility: There, but for the grace of God, go I.

Yes, it feels good (temporarily) to point fingers and divide the world into tidy little groups of good and bad. Getting boundaries right is one of ego's major challenges, in fact. If it isn't setting up false barriers as a way to protect and build itself up, it's off on the other end of the spectrum, blurring boundaries in a misguided attempt to merge with the other. With ego at the helm, we careen back and forth from rigid boundaries to *no* boundaries, in an endless loop of aversion and craving.

The middle point between these two extremes is a sort of "semi-permeable membrane" (to borrow a term from high school biology) – a boundary that maintains the integrity of the cell and yet allows for give and take across the barrier.

True intimacy requires a delicate balancing act of relating freely and fully to others, while still remaining firmly anchored in the security and wholeness of the Authentic Self. To tell the truth, it ain't easy, and few of us get it right.

Differentiation vs. emotional fusion

The poet Rainer Maria Rilke described the paradox of intimacy this way: "A merging of two people is an impossibility, and where it seems to exist, it is a hemming-in, a mutual consent that robs one party or both parties of their fullest freedom and development. But once the realization is accepted that even between the closest people infinite distances exist, a marvelous living side-by-side can grow up for them, if they succeed in loving the expanse between them, which gives them the possibility of always seeing each other as a whole and before an immense sky."

The challenge of intimacy is to show up consistently as your Authentic Self in relationship – and the more intimate the relationship, the more difficult that is to do. This is why psychologist and relationship expert David Schnarch describes marriage as the best "people-growing machine" there is. His classic book *Passionate Marriage* describes the process of **differentiation** that is the essential foundation for every truly intimate relationship, romantic or otherwise.

Differentiation requires immense courage and honesty. Not only do you have to hold on tightly to your Authentic Self, but you also have to be willing for your partner to do the same. This can feel like very risky behavior, because we're used to holding on tightly to the *other*. Ego, fueled as always by fear, makes demands of the partner: Do this and this and this, so that I will know you love me, and then I'll love you back. And if you don't, I will withhold my love from you. This is **emotional fusion**, the only kind of relationship many of us know.

With emotional fusion, like Siamese twins, there are no clear boundaries between the parties. A constant, subtle (or not so subtle) dance of "push me – pull you" provides the backdrop for most interactions. In an emotionally fused relationship, both partners unconsciously manipulate the other in an effort to feel validated for who they are and what they want. They hand the responsibility for fulfilling their needs over to their partner and then feel justified in making demands that masquerade as requests. (If you're wondering whether you do this, ask yourself, "Would I really be okay if the answer was no?")

This is *other-validated* intimacy, which is what most of us equate with love. Being validated by significant others is great when it's offered freely, but it becomes a problem when you *need* it in order to feel okay about yourself and your relationship. When you don't get the validation you think you need from your partner, anxiety rises.... and then the next domino falls. You make your partner responsible for soothing your anxiety, since s/he is clearly in the wrong. You expect an apology, a change in behavior, a validation of your position and needs. And the entire pattern hinges on a deep-seated unwillingness in both partners to confront their own triggers and behavior.

In a differentiated relationship, you can and should ask for what you want, as long as you're fully prepared for the answer to be no. In *self-validated* intimacy, you're not a doormat, repressing emotions and desires to counterfeit enlightenment. This is very important! If you're anything like me, you feel a strong temptation to take the supposed "high road" and sweep your real, messy feelings and wishes under the rug in the name of peace and harmony. Note to self: It doesn't work. And, more important, it's not intimacy.

Differentiation involves three key skills: self-confrontation, self-validation and self-soothing. (Notice that it's all about yourself, and not about your partner.) Let's look at each one. The first is **self-confrontation**, which could also be called self-honesty or awareness. It requires you to look within first, at your own motivation and agenda, your own triggers and patterns of behavior, rather than automatically looking for someone else to blame. (If this sounds familiar, then good. I've been doing my job.)

Self-validation is then standing up and asking *explicitly* for your own needs and desires (rather than manipulating others covertly), and ultimately accepting the responsibility for fulfilling them yourself if your partner is not willing or able to. And finally, because doing the previous two things will inevitably make you feel very anxious, **self-soothing** is the ability to tolerate that discomfort and calm your own anxiety, rather than expecting your partner to do it for you.

Dr. Schnarch makes two things clear that you might find as hard to swallow as I did. First, we emerge from our families of origin at about the same level of differentiation our parents achieved, and many people never progress beyond that. Second, we always choose a mate at around the same level of differentiation as ourselves. Yep. So if you're in a troubled relationship and looking for a scapegoat, you won't find one here. The happy news is that this is precisely the reason why marriage is such a good people-growing machine. We unconsciously choose exactly the people who can help us grow the most, provided that we're willing to do the work.

The reason that emotional fusion can be so difficult to recognize and break out of is that it is fully reciprocal. Most marriages operate like a well-oiled – albeit dysfunctional – machine. As Schnarch writes, "Fusion ties people together like a single emotional network that allows anxiety to flow readily from one member to the next." (Remember that anxiety is also the prime fuel driving the Victim Triangle – and ego.)

However, if even one partner is willing to do the work of becoming differentiated, the other will either have to change in response or the relationship will naturally come to an end. Whenever you choose soul over ego, there's an inevitable ripple effect in every one of your relationships, and in the world at large... it's that powerful.

Here's Schnarch one more time: "Intimacy involves your 'relationship with yourself' as well as your relationship with your partner. [...] Self-validated intimacy is the means to *two* ends: becoming more of a person and developing a more resilient intimate relationship." Holding on to your Authentic Self – developing the honesty to confront your own behavior, the courage to validate your own needs and desires, and the inner strength to soothe your own anxiety – means that you're no longer setting yourself the impossible task of controlling other people's behavior in order to feel okay about yourself.

In other words, you're living from the soul's agenda and not the ego's. Well done, there.

Only when one is connected to one's core is one connected to others...
~ *Anne Morrow Lindbergh*

We all have a better guide in ourselves, if we would attend to it, than any other person can be.
~ *Jane Austen*

CHAPTER THREE
Work

This is the true joy in life, the being used for a purpose recognized by yourself as a mighty one, the being thoroughly worn out before being thrown on the scrap heap, the being a force of nature instead of a feverish selfish little clod of ailments and grievances complaining that the world will not devote itself to making you happy.
~ George Bernard Shaw

I don't know about you, but being a "feverish selfish little clod of ailments and grievances" doesn't sound too appealing to me. Like many people, I have a love/hate relationship with work. Mostly I fantasize about having endless leisure, but when I get it life can come to feel flat and pointless in a remarkably short period of time. What's going on here?

I believe it's the difference between work and *dharma*. Dharma is a Sanskrit word with multiple meanings, among them "path of righteousness" and "right way of living." In the

West, we've restricted the idea of work to mean career or job, and tied it inexorably with the earning of money and status. Not surprisingly, this is where ego comes into the picture. It would serve us better to consider our work in the world from a broader perspective.

When you hear the word "calling," what comes to mind? What about "purpose?" These are other concepts that often enter into the discussion about work; concepts that are closer to the soul's perspective but that can also muddy the waters if we aren't careful. Does your work necessarily have to be your calling? Can you fulfill your purpose in life while working at a less than ideal job? And just where *does* money fit in when we're talking about soul? It's complicated to mix the spiritual and the vocational, which is why most of us prefer to keep them in firmly separated compartments.

Work is where we spend the bulk of our waking hours (whether or not we're officially employed outside the home) and where we derive a large part of our identity. I know this, since I used to have an easy label to apply to myself – physical therapist – and now when I'm asked what I "do," I stammer around from

writer to editor to meditation teacher to...
hmmm. It's uncomfortable not to have a readily
available, socially acceptable (better yet,
impressive) work identity to hang your hat on in
social situations.

In addition, work often nearly *forces* us into
our Social Selves, since being truly authentic on
the job can have negative consequences if it's
not handled skillfully. We're encouraged to keep
a tight lid on emotions, to avoid the appearance
of weakness or personal trouble at all cost, to
project an unwavering image of competence and
confidence. And finally, the intrinsic hierarchy
of the working world makes it nearly impossible
not to see others as "separate," whether they're
bosses or employees, clients or competition.

Where, oh where, is the place for soul in all
of this?

Making meaning

The heart of this discussion lies in how we
assign meaning in our lives. Although *making
meaning* is one of the most fundamental of
human activities, too often we're completely
unconscious of the process. Yet the meaning we
give to work – or any other activity – can

transform our experience of it, regardless of the activity itself.

The classic folk tale of the three stonecutters illustrates this. A man walking along a road comes upon a busy building site, where many laborers are cutting and shaping great blocks of stone. When he asks the first person he sees why he's working so hard, the man snarls, "What do you think? I have to do *something* to keep from starving, and that cursed supervisor makes us work like dogs." A second worker replies cheerfully, "Me – I like seeing how fast I can cut the stone, and I'm happy to be able to feed my family doing an honest day's work." The third laborer the man approaches says with pride, "Don't you see? I'm building a cathedral!"

From the soul's perspective, no activity is *inherently* more meaningful than another, although ego will tell you differently. I've spent a lot of time thinking about this, especially as I've entered the second half of my life. Often, the demanding agenda of the first half of life – acquiring an education, figuring out how to pay the bills, possibly raising a family – supplies its own sense of meaning, or at least keeps us busy enough not to question it too much. This often drops away in mid-life, leaving many people high and dry, without a compelling answer to the big questions: "What's my life all about? Why am I even here?" Cue the mid-life crisis.

Here are some of the things I've puzzled out in the past few years of my own mid-life crisis. First, it helps to define *for yourself* what your version of a meaningful life is. Start by making a list of activities that feel meaningful to you. My list includes things like: helping others, spending time in nature, learning something new, being creative. Yours might be completely different, which is exactly the point. Absolutely anything is allowed on the list as long as it feels meaningful to you, and it doesn't have to be lofty, either. Just plain old "having fun" is also on my list.

Then try to formulate a more general statement of purpose, or adopt someone else's statement that resonates with you. I like this one from therapist and writer Katherine Woodward Thomas: "What makes life worth living is being actively engaged in becoming the finest, most delicious human being you can possibly be in this lifetime. What makes life worth living is finding people and projects that you can love and stand by and give yourself to completely."

You can see that nothing in this statement is dependent upon having a particular job or life situation or level of income. This definition bypasses the ego entirely and gets directly to the soul level of meaning making. Why are you here? What makes a life successful? Is it even possible for a life to be *un*successful?

I tend to think not. My gut tells me that no life is unsuccessful, first because we have no idea of the true impact of anyone's life and second because the very definitions of success and failure are so tied up with the ego's agenda. Many, many philosophers and teachers have questioned our eagerness to rank ourselves and others in terms of importance or worthiness. Remember Jesus saying that the first will be last and the last will be first?

This is both deeply cautionary and wildly liberating. *It takes the pressure of comparison off the table.* I don't get to feel superior, but I also don't have to feel inferior to anyone. We're all on our own different paths, not further ahead or behind on the same path. It also turns everything that we do on its head, since we've literally turned the measuring stick upside down.

I think one way to put this into practice is to do "small things as if they were great, and great things as if they were small" (to paraphrase the philosopher Blaise Pascal). In other words, it's not the activity itself that matters, but the way in which it is approached. You can perform menial tasks as if they were a great honor and privilege – this is parenting in a nutshell – and approach lofty tasks with grace and humility. Both of these are an affront to ego, which chafes at lowly tasks and craves the recognition of anything "high profile."

Ego judges success and failure by external forms like title and paycheck (doing), while soul focuses on the essence of the experience (being), not the form. You could be a janitor with great love and care, or a titan of industry with anger and hatred – or vice versa. You could meet an addict in a halfway house or the leader of the free world, and the external form itself would tell you nothing about the internal state of that person.

This inner/outer focus is central to the soul/ego divide. The Social Self automatically sizes up relative worth based on looks, status, achievement, power and so on. It's one of the most subtle and pernicious prejudices we hold, no matter how much lip service we pay to its opposite, and we're especially harsh in applying those standards to ourselves. We have to let ourselves off the ego hook first, before we can extend that same mercy to others.

To do that we have to embrace our own intrinsic worth as human *beings*, irrespective of what we do or achieve in the world. And that's a tall order.

To be or not to be

This being vs. doing discussion has been going on non-stop for millennia. Recently I've been running my own personal experiments on the topic in the form of an overwhelming compulsion to "waste" time. This is easy to do when you work for yourself from home, trust me.

I can spend a whole afternoon napping on the couch. I research strange and probably useless subjects on the Internet. I regularly find myself on the floor playing five or ten games of Solitaire (yes, I still use a real deck of cards). And while I do, the demons of ego present themselves to me one by one to disarm. They say things like, "What a loser!" and "You'll never accomplish anything" and "You're wasting your life."

My job, as I see it, is to stare them down. I don't fear that I'll always be napping and playing Solitaire (more on that later), but right now my job is to grapple with these ego demons who try to convince me that my worth as a human being comes from being "productive." My soul tells me that my worth is intrinsic and inviolable, that I am no less loved nor worthy of love if I never produce a single thing in my lifetime.

How could it be otherwise? If it weren't true, what would we make of the people who for one reason or another (physical or mental illness, incarceration or other lack of freedom, extreme poverty, to name a few) *can't* be productive in the worldly sense? Are they worthless because of that? You often hear people say, "What a waste of life!" but is it really? Is an outwardly unproductive life wasted? Are more productive people more worthy? Ego would say yes, and I think that many of us would agree on some level. We certainly hold *ourselves* to that standard, if not others.

The nature of time itself enters into this discussion (we're going to get metaphysical here for a moment). Is it even possible to waste something that, depending on the way you look at it, either doesn't actually exist or exists in literally endless quantity? Can you waste something that it's impossible to run out of? Maybe I have an advantage here because I believe in reincarnation, which removes the pressure of thinking that we only have one life in which to "get it right" and make our mark, as it were.

I don't want to step on any toes, but it occurs to me that the traditionally Christian view of life is rather ego-oriented in this sense. I just find it hard to believe that God would really be disappointed in me for playing Solitaire rather than writing ten pages of my book. It might even be that grappling with those demons was the *most* productive use of my time. Can we really know?

Ironically, I often find that periods of seeming unproductivity lead to bursts of creativity, which is why I don't worry too much that I'll end up Dumpster-diving for a living. When I divest work of its moral weightiness and sense of imperative, usually it turns out to be very pleasant. If we approach it simply and naturally, work itself feels simple and natural. No big deal, just what we do as (temporarily) physical beings in a physical world. We can hold it more lightly, whether it's rocket science or sweeping the floor or making a sales call. It doesn't have to define us or signal our relative worth to society and ourselves.

And when we take this stance, we suddenly find that all of our moments are equally precious and important. Because the corollary to believing that greater productivity equals greater worth is that we then degrade or dismiss a good chunk of our lives. The peak moments (when you receive an award or promotion, for example) are seen as "better" or more important than all the little ordinary moments leading up to them. Talk about a waste of life!

Even the biggest celebrities and the most powerful players in the world spend the majority of their lives doing fairly mundane things like sleeping, eating, bathing and dressing. No one lives on a permanent high. (That would be pretty exhausting anyway.) Annie Dillard wrote, "How we spend our days is, of course, how we spend our lives. What we do with this hour, and that one, is what we are doing." When we follow ego, putting a premium on some hours and devaluing the rest, we essentially devalue our lives.

It's the classic journey vs. destination conundrum. Do we enjoy the path itself, or just the reward at the end? Are we living each moment that's available to us, or only some of them? You can guess where ego and soul weigh in on those questions. When you're fixated on reaching a destination, you essentially vacate the present moment in favor of some moment in the future. And, just like opening presents on Christmas morning, that moment of arrival is all too fleeting. And then it's on to something else, in a never-ending race for the next peak experience.

But what happens when we stop? It sounds a bit limp and passive to sit around simply *be*-ing all the time. Let's say that you've made the commitment to live in the moment, to enjoy the path, to be and not just do: Is there still a role for aspiration and goal setting in your life? Is it possible to think big and do big without automatically falling into the ego's agenda?

What about your calling or purpose in life – that Holy Grail so many of us are searching for?

Now that we've established that you don't *have* to do anything to prove your worth, let's talk about what you *want* to do.

Dharma

We'll start with the good news: Your calling is also a path, not a destination. In this sense, you don't "find" your calling; you live it, one step at a time. This is also the bad news, at least to ego, because ego loves certainty. Ego is looking desperately for that *one sure thing* that will make everything else fall perfectly into place for the rest of your life: "So that's what I'm supposed to be doing!" Sigh of relief.

Callings don't work that way. They are slippery things that morph and develop as we do (which is actually a lot more fun in the end). And they don't respond well to ego's favorite henchmen: strategizing and effort. You are far more likely to live out your calling using the soul's methods of *intention* and *inspired action*.

In the most fundamental sense, I believe that each of us has a calling to live out our true selves. That's why your calling will always arise organically from what is truest in yourself, not from anything outside. You can attempt to take on a calling, either because of external pressure or from a desire to emulate someone else, but I don't believe it will ever truly be satisfying when that is the case.

So a good place to start is in doing the things you love to do. They don't necessarily have to be the things you're good at – although that helps – but they must light you up inside. If you're still not sure whether you're heading in the "right" direction, just begin with the clear intention to live what is truest in yourself. My belief is that whenever we set and hold an intention, the universe answers. Sometimes we don't recognize the answer when it comes, and sometimes we don't like it at first, but it's not possible to hold an intention steadily without setting the wheels of the universe in motion.

Very often the process of answering takes a long time. In fact, you could even say that the process of answering – as long as you continue to hold the intention – is the calling itself! We're usually in such a hurry (ego again). Ego wants results yesterday, but growing into your calling is the work of a lifetime. In his book *The*

Great Work of Your Life, Stephen Cope describes dharma, or calling, as "truth" and goes on to write, "Yogis believe that our greatest responsibility in life is to this inner possibility – this dharma – and they believe that every human being's duty is to utterly, fully, and completely embody his own idiosyncratic dharma."

The yogic tradition also has a lot to say about the kind of doing that I call *inspired action*. As Cope puts it: "… the most sublime kind of doing is really a perfect expression of authentic being." I love that! Here's how inspired action works in my life: I set an intention, and then I wait to see what wants to happen. Is that clear as mud? How do you know what "wants to happen?" The clues are both internal and external. First, listen to any urges you have, no matter how strange or unrelated to your intention they might seem. If possible, act on them, at least with some small baby steps. Then watch how the universe responds. Are doors opening? Walk through them. If they're closing, stop and wait. It might only be a question of timing, or another door altogether might unexpectedly open.

Do you see how this path is almost more like an intricate maze than the well-lighted superhighway your ego craves? You can't chart out this path, but you can make the whole journey a few baby steps at a time. I've learned a lot about this in my writing process. I start with an idea and a basic structure (my intention) and then I write a bit and watch what happens. Often the writing flows smoothly for a while and then suddenly grinds to a halt. I know there's something that wants to be said, but I can't quite pin it down.

When that happens, I stop writing rather than trying to push through. (I've tried pushing through and inevitably what I write is awful.) Usually the most fruitful thing I can do is something completely unrelated. I don't try to puzzle or "effort" it out, although when ideas float up naturally I'll sit down right away and get them on paper. Sometimes I put a project away for weeks at a time, and when I'm eventually inspired to pick it up again the words often pour out.

I've conceptualized this process as the children's game of "red light/green light" and trained myself to pay close attention to those internal and external signals. When you first start playing this game, your ego will scream that you should stop being passive and get to work *making things happen*. Does that sound familiar? But I've found that inspired action, if I wait for it, is incredibly efficient. I'd rather spend five hours playing Solitaire (not really, I swear) and thirty minutes writing productively than five hours writing something that ends up in the trash.

Yes, I agree that it's easier to put this concept into action when you work for yourself in a creative field, but it can be adapted to a more conventional work situation, and certainly to your life in general. We all know what it's like to try to force something to happen that just doesn't want to be. How bloodied do you have to get banging your head against a locked door before you look for one that's open? This is about fitting yourself into the flow of life, rather than trying to force life to flow in the channels *you* cut for it. Much, much easier, believe me.

This is the true essence of dharma: It's a way of both being and doing in the world that honors *who you are* and the reality of what is *actually happening*. These two things aren't subject to your ego's desire to change them, however much your ego wishes they were. Psychologist Gay Hendricks wrote, "Thinking we can change the unchangeable is the cunning trick the ego plays on us to allow it to stay in control." If we could really understand that, deep down, almost every single problem we think we have would cease to be a problem. Now that sounds like a Holy Grail worth searching for, doesn't it?

As usual, the ego tends to complicate things that are simple and straightforward to soul. From the soul's perspective, being and doing, work and life, aren't inscrutable puzzles to solve, but simply two different ways of showing up in the world as your Authentic Self. "Calling" is not some fabled destination to reach, but a journey of authenticity that is lived out moment to moment. And money (I told you we'd get to money), well...

Money is just energy
I don't pretend to have all of my own money issues sorted out, but I do know that, when I approach money simply and straightforwardly as energy, I'm at least headed in the right

direction. Although it has a reputation as the "root of all evil," money truly is a neutral force with equal potential to be a problem and a blessing (and will most likely play both of these roles at some point or other in your lifetime).

Now, obviously, I'm not addressing the issue of extreme poverty here, and I ask your indulgence for approaching this discussion as one of those privileged First World "problems." We're basically talking about a feeling of lack here that most of the world would consider fantastical abundance. I totally get that.

Nevertheless, money occupies a special place in most people's minds, whether they're fabulously rich or just scraping by, so it pays (get it?) to examine your relationship with it. The main point I want to make is that money is a *spiritual substance*, just like everything else in the universe. There's nothing unholy about it, and your soul doesn't take any particular satisfaction from watching you struggle, heroically or otherwise. If you equate poverty with moral superiority, that belief is not serving you well. (And it's a common belief.)

If we want the energy of money flowing into our lives, we definitely have to purge ourselves of any overt or covert beliefs that money is bad, or that people who have a lot of money are bad. One way I got over that was to say to myself, "I will never be poor enough to make someone else rich." (Just as being sick yourself will never make anyone else healthy.) Money is not a zero-sum game.

On the other hand, if I were rich I would theoretically have the capacity to help others in a much bigger way. And incidentally, giving regularly happens to be a great way to increase the flow of energy toward yourself as well. Gratitude will do that too. What doesn't help? Complaining, even in a joking way, about how broke you are. Keep your attention on what you have, not what you lack, and it will grow. That's my Law of Attraction plug for the day.

I won't spend a lot more time on money here, because there are already some wonderful resources available on the subject (a favorite is appropriately called *The Soul of Money* by Lynne Twist). I truly believe that when you make the choice for soul, the other things in life, including money, tend to sort themselves out. Not that you'll suddenly win the lottery and nothing bad will ever happen to you, or even that you'll always get what you *think* you need. But what you *really* need in every situation will be there for you. True freedom and peace of mind come when you trust that life itself is kind, that you are safe and loved no matter what. No amount of money in the bank will give you that kind of guarantee.

There is literally no part of life, including money, that's exempt or apart from soul. Remember that ego likes to create separation, but with soul it's really all one thing, and that one thing is love. When your work – or dharma – becomes an expression of that love and the Authentic Self within you, the energy of the entire universe will support you in that.

The true profession of a man is to find his way to himself.
~Hermann Hesse

One must be something in order to do something.
~ Goethe

What a long time it can take to become the person one has always been! How often in the process we mask ourselves in faces that are not our own. How much dissolving and shaking of ego we must endure before we discover our deep identity – the true self within every human being that is the seed of authentic vocation.

~ *Parker Palmer*

CHAPTER FOUR
Adventure & Play

We wholly overlook the essential fact that the achievements which society rewards are won at the cost of diminution of personality. Many – far too many – aspects of life which should also have been experienced lie in the lumber room among dusty memories.
~ Carl Jung

In the West we work hard, and then we often go one step further and turn play into just another version of work. It's an unfortunate truth that the ego is sadly lacking in playfulness and adventure. To play with abandon, to create, to learn and grow and stretch out in a new direction, you have to be willing to set aside your dignity and even look a bit foolish, which ego does very reluctantly, if at all.

Ego is heavily invested in appearing cool and in control at all times, which is seriously limiting. When you need to look like an expert in every single situation, every single moment of your life, it's impossible to ever let your guard down. This is an exhausting and ultimately unsatisfying way to live.

Consider what happens throughout our lifetimes. As small children we're relatively free of the Social Self, as discussed in Chapter One. To put it succinctly, little kids don't give a rat's ass if they look foolish to anyone else. This quickly changes in elementary school. That's when we start censoring ourselves and only doing the things we have a good chance of doing well. One or two episodes of schoolyard shaming will cure you very thoroughly of any desire to "put yourself out there." Even writing that floods me with remembered dread and panic!

The social armor we first develop as children keeps us living small and safe, but soul is beckoning us out of the corner and into a much broader and more joyous (albeit possibly scarier) life. In *The Hero Within,* Carol S. Pearson writes: "There is a certain level of danger inherent in the hero's journey that awakens our souls. The ego desperately wants safety. The soul wants to live. The truth is, we cannot lead a real life without risk."

Remember that ego is fear-based, and as such security is its top priority. Ego is inherently conservative and risk averse, only taking the bets that look like a sure thing. The irony is that security, like ego itself, is simply an illusion anyway. As Helen Keller said, "Security is mostly a superstition. It doesn't exist in nature... life is either a daring adventure or nothing."

That daring adventure is what your soul is calling you to. Most of us have a love/hate relationship with adventure. We like it in theory but often hate it in practice, because it's scary. And uncomfortable. And we don't know how it's going to turn out. When adventure comes knocking we're likely to say, like Bilbo Baggins in *The Hobbit*, "Sorry! I don't want any adventures. Not today." We're seduced by comfort and familiarity, and wake up a few decades later wondering what happened. And that's the problem in a nutshell: Nothing happened.

Henry David Thoreau wrote, "It is remarkable how few events or crises there are in our histories; how little exercised we have been in our minds; how few experiences we have had. [...] It would be well, if all our lives were a divine tragedy even, instead of this trivial comedy or farce."

That's a 19th century description of the feeling we have come to know as: *Meh*. Not exactly terrible, but not very inspiring either. I'm confident that deep down most of us would rather live a life of adventure and growth and zest and joy and playfulness, if only we could figure out how to get free of the straitjacket ego has us in. Well, I am here to help. If you want to open up your life to adventure (and you should), there are basically two ways to approach it:

- Make a practice of deliberately getting out of your comfort zone (in other words, go looking for adventure).
- Learn to stop resisting the adventure that life hands you.

Let's take a look at them both.

The case for pulling out your own rug
I love this image, which I borrowed from the Buddhist nun Pema Chödrön. It's one thing (and not a very comfortable thing) to have the rug pulled out from under you, but quite

another to pull out your own rug. That takes real courage, and maybe a little bit of craziness too. The poet Rumi said, "Run from what's comfortable. Forget safety. Live where you fear to live. Destroy your reputation. Be notorious. I have tried prudent planning long enough. From now on I'll be mad."

Although I admire his commitment, pulling out your own rug doesn't necessarily have to involve feats of obvious derring-do. It can be as simple as introducing yourself to the new person in the office, even though you feel really shy and awkward. Or going to the movie alone when you really want to see it and no one else is available. It's saying the hard thing that needs to be said. It's anything that nudges out your boundaries, even a little bit, and expands your comfort zone beyond where it was before. It's staring down the feelings of fear and uncertainty that ego uses to keep you in your own familiar lane. Going ahead and jumping even when you're not positive you'll land well (or you're certain you won't!).

No matter what ego says, life doesn't come with guarantees of success. You can do every sensible thing that ego and society and your mother tell you to do, and still end up a hot mess. It happens all the time, as a matter of fact. We want so much to believe that there's a formula we can follow that will keep us safe and happy. There is, but it's not the one you think. The true formula lies in giving up the *need to know* and embracing the exhilaration of uncertainty. Abandoning the constant quest for security in favor of the opportunity to stretch and grow.

In short, choosing the perspective of soul over ego. Love over fear. Love is the perfect guide to follow when setting out into unknown territory. The soul speaks through those little nudges of curiosity and intrigue and delight. Follow them. Think in baby steps if you want to calm your fears. What's the smallest step you can take in the direction that intrigues you the most? Take it, and then wait to see what happens. Be a scientist. Get your curiosity going. Make it a game to see where the path leads, and don't take it all so seriously! Ego can be such a drama queen. Soul feels light and easy.

Let who you are at the core of your core come out in all its quirkiness. Nothing has to "make sense." This is not about taking marketing classes to help you get your business to the next level – unless, of course, marketing lights your hair on fire. In that case, have at it. Never buy into the myth that you're too old or too busy or too *anything* to embrace adventure. Even reading in a different genre than you usually choose will shake things up in there. Poke into a new store or restaurant. Check out the Meetup groups in your area, which will get you meeting new people as well as trying new activities.

Pulling out your own rug is far more of an attitude and an orientation to life than it is any specific thing that you do. It's a way of staying alive and fresh and open to life. If you live this way, you can keep growing and changing right up to the moment you die. Resolve to be one of those old people we've all met who astonish with the force of their passion and interest in life.

Become aware of the filters that you automatically use to screen your experience, and question them. Some of them are probably legitimate. If you're an introvert like me, you probably hate large parties with lots of noise and small talk. There are other ways to mix with new people that will suit you better. However, I'm betting that many of your filters are arbitrary or outdated and can safely be tossed. Maybe you're avoiding a section of your city that has long since changed, or perhaps there's an activity you tried and disliked in your youth that you might love today.

As Henry Miller put it: "Develop interest in life as you see it; in people, things, literature, music – the world is so rich, simply throbbing with rich treasures, beautiful souls and interesting people. Forget yourself." Or, at least, forget all the strictures and prejudices your Social Self has developed over the years. Let some fresh air into your life.

Getting out of your comfort zone actually becomes quite addictive once you get used to it. I think it must be very like the adrenaline high that keeps people doing extreme sports. You can build up this adventure muscle by exercising it, so that it becomes easier and easier to pull out your own rug. The safety of the rug is an illusion anyway. Life can and will pull it out for you if you don't do it yourself (and even when you do). That's when you get to practice the second kind of adventuring, which is whole-hearted surrender to what life brings.

Surrender

Okay, so this kind of adventure is a lot harder to embrace, because it's not something we go out and choose. Sometimes it's thrilling and welcome: An unexpected job offer, or a new relationship that comes out of the blue. But often it's not: Illness. Divorce. Death of a loved one. Loss of a job. Some "adventures," right?

We'll be talking about how the soul uses these dark times for growth in the next chapter, but for now we'll focus on the first and most crucial step in the process, which is both as simple and as impossible as giving up your resistance to what life brings. You might not love it, but it happened. What to do with it? Not what to do *about* it, but what, if anything, can you make of it?

A book that hit me right between the eyes was *The Surrender Experiment* by Michael Singer. The author decided some forty plus years ago that he would basically say "yes" to any situation that life handed him. This included returning from vacation to find someone building a house for themselves on his rural property. After struggling a bit with the voice in his head (ego, naturally) Singer rolled up his sleeves and helped to finish the house. I won't spoil the story for you, but it gets even weirder than that, and it completely upended my understanding of how far it's possible to take the practice of surrender.

Let me hasten to add that Michael Singer was undertaking a full-on spiritual journey at the same time he ran his "surrender experiment." Obviously, without that context, surrendering can be a potentially dysfunctional reaction to stressful or harmful situations. Surrender as Singer practiced it, and as I'm advocating here, is more of a willing participation with the flow of life as it occurs. It's a conscious, sustained effort to remove ego from the driver's seat and let soul take the wheel.

I like the metaphor of driving a bus, so let's explore that further. Ego, of course, wants to drive. For most people, ego drives the bus their entire lives. Some people do manage to get ego out of the driver's seat, at least part of the time – but even then it's usually standing right there, obsessively giving directions, anxiously tracking the route, ready to grab the wheel back at any time. It's a rare person who gets his or her ego to actually sit down in the back of the bus and enjoy the ride. And *that's* what I mean by "surrender."

I love that Singer took issue with the voice in his head. It makes me think of that classic declaration of defiance: "You're not the boss of me!" Who *is* the boss of you? Well, if you're not even aware that you have a voice in your head, you can be sure that it's the boss. You have to be aware of it before you can even hope to question it. The best way to become aware of it is through a regular practice of meditation, which doesn't have to be anything more complicated than sitting quietly in a chair with your eyes closed and your mind open.

The more familiar you become with the voice in your head, the more easily you'll recognize your own patterns of resistance to life. Usually my inner voice's first response to just about *anything* is resistance. Even the supposedly fun stuff! It's an everyday exercise for me to observe the resistance, which feels like a clenching up in my chest, and then to deliberately choose to open and release. Over and over again: I feel the clenching, I take a deep breath, I deliberately relax and open. Deep breaths help (lots of them).

This opening up to life as it actually happens is the real adventure. Ask yourself, as Michael Singer did, "... what would happen if we respected the flow of life and used our free will to participate in what's unfolding, instead of fighting it?" Imagine how much energy we could free up by releasing our constant resistance to reality, from the long red light to the scary diagnosis. Resistance is exhausting, as well as futile. It depletes the energy we could otherwise use to respond in a creative and life-affirming way.

As you quiet the voice of resistance (ego), you also create space to hear the whispers of soul. Paramahansa Yogananda says in the classic *Autobiography of a Yogi*: "Intuition is soul guidance, appearing naturally in man during those instants when his mind is calm." There's a term for the mind that's open, calm and receptive to soul's guidance: Beginner's Mind. As you can imagine, ego wants nothing to do with it.

Beginner's Mind

According to Alexander Pope, "Some people never learn anything because they understand everything too quickly." That's ego for you, the perennial expert. Beginner's Mind is fluid and supple, open to many possibilities, while the expert's mind is often hampered by preconceptions. In Taoism it is said: "To attain knowledge, add things everyday. To attain wisdom, remove things everyday." Once again, the way of soul is paradoxical.

Cultivating Beginner's Mind is the perfect way to approach adventure and learning. It's like being a child again, willing to look foolish, willing to "waste time" just noodling around, eager to pursue new ideas and experiences. Beginner's Mind isn't jaded or rigid or defensive. Unlike ego, it can afford to take creative risks because it doesn't have an image to protect. It's not trying to prove anything.

With Beginner's Mind, you are free to try anything. Failure isn't possible, because the goal is not to succeed, but to learn through the process. Science fiction writer Kurt Vonnegut, Jr. wrote: "... practice any art, music, singing, dancing, acting, drawing, painting, sculpting, poetry, fiction, essays, reportage, no matter how well or how badly, not to get money and fame, but to experience *becoming*, to find out what's inside you, to *make your soul grow.*" (His emphasis.)

Whatever you do that stretches you in any way enriches your spirit, no matter how insignificant or irrelevant (to the ego) it might seem. It isn't irrelevant to soul. Don't rest on your laurels. It's so easy to find the things that we're good at and then stop there. There might be twenty more things that you're good at that you'll never discover if you don't keep trying new ones. Research has shown that our gray matter is way more plastic than we used to believe. Novel experiences physically re-wire your brain with new connections and pathways. Try to use *all* of your brain, not just the small percentage that you've practiced the most.

We were born to learn and create; it's part of what makes us human. But there's a secret to unleashing the power of creativity: You need consistency to really get it flowing. That seems counter to the popular myth of the undisciplined, free-spirited creator, but it's true. Make it a habit – set an intention – to be creative. It primes the pump and opens the channels for inspiration to flow.

It also helps to put *in* the right food for your soul to grow on. I truly love this quote from the Bible and try to live by it: "… whatever is true, whatever is honorable, whatever is right, whatever is pure, whatever is lovely, whatever is of good repute, if there is any excellence and if anything is worthy of praise, let your mind dwell on these things."

This pretty much leaves out most of what's on TV, including the news. More than a century ago my favorite philosopher, Henry David Thoreau, wrote: "Read not the *Times*. Read the Eternities." Feed yourself what is nourishing to your spirit. Hang around people who make your heart sing. Be picky about what and who you let into your life.

Our souls also need rest and quiet to grow. Time in nature. Even a large helping of boredom, which I've heard called the "fertile void." When your schedule is jam-packed, there's no opening for inspiration to strike. If you're listening to music, for instance, try to really *listen* to it, or turn it off and listen to the silence. We fill every single moment of our lives with sound and activity. Hurry, hurry, hurry, the ego says. It likes feeling important and popular and plugged in. Carl Jung said, "Hurry is not of the devil; it *is* the devil."

We need to give our souls space and time to stretch out. Do you remember how long and leisurely a summer day was when you were a kid (if you were lucky, that is)? When was the last time you had a whole day with absolutely nothing scheduled? Would you feel anxious if you did? I was in the hospital once in Germany, where they not only don't rush you out, they keep you longer than you think you need. The week I spent there, in a room alone at the end of the hall, was one of the most exquisite of my life (aside from the small matter of being unwell). For long, long mornings and afternoons and evenings I lay in bed, doing essentially nothing but watching the shadows cross the wall. I didn't even think after a while. I just *was*. Does it really take sickness to remove ourselves from ego's death grip?

Illness is one of the more drastic methods soul will use to pry us away from ego, but we don't have to let it go that far. Body sensations and emotions provide a built-in sensor that lets us monitor our connection to soul. We are spirits walking around in meat suits, and the meat suits actually *matter*. They aren't just afterthoughts or inconveniences to overcome, but sophisticated tools that can help us navigate this physical reality as spiritual beings. If you're serious about soul growth, you simply can't afford to ignore this connection between body and spirit.

The connection goes both ways, too: What you do with your body impacts your spirit as much as the other way around. In a sense, the body is like a fractal or microcosm of the universe itself. When we tend our bodies – our own personal patch of physical reality – we're also tending the universe and everything in it. Learning to skillfully operate these miraculous tools we've been given is the ultimate in "extreme adventures." Outer space isn't really the final frontier (sorry, Captain Kirk) – inner space is.

The mind/body/spirit connection

The meat suit you wear – your body – is really a walking, talking vibrational field that receives and broadcasts energy with incredible sensitivity. This may seem weird at first, because reality appears to be so solid (both our bodies and the so-called "real world" around us), but if you think about how your physical senses actually process the world, you'll realize that it's all vibration: Light waves tell you what you see, sound waves tell you what you hear, vibrations against touch receptors tell you what you feel, and so on. It's all energy or vibrations in various forms, including your very own body.

When you shift your awareness from the apparent solidity of the physical world to its vibrational basis, you suddenly gain a much bigger view of the world and how you relate to it, both internally and externally. The vibrational world feels a lot more fluid, and you begin to realize how your thoughts, intentions and feelings (all energy) influence both your body and the world around you in a continuous positive feedback loop. It's very exciting, actually! Your vibrational frequency changes as you continue to grow your connection to soul, becoming clearer and more powerful. You feel this energy yourself, and so do the people around you.

There are several aspects of this to explore. One that relates very specifically to soul growth is the fact that you can't just work on your spirit and ignore the container that holds it. In this experience as human beings we are both spiritual and physical, fully divine and fully human. To be balanced and truly thrive, we must be both **open** (to spirit) and **grounded** (in our bodies and in the present moment/situation). Many people who choose a spiritual path are very open, but not at all grounded. Some people, especially serious athletes, may be very grounded (at least while engaging in their sports) but not at all open. And the majority of people, sadly, are neither open nor grounded.

Some extreme moments, like near death experiences or times of great danger, offer a spontaneous taste of being open and grounded at the same time. People who have experienced these situations describe time slowing down, being extraordinarily aware of sounds and sights and physical sensations, and experiencing a sense of absolute safety and well-being in the knowledge that they are surrounded and held in a loving energy field. These things are theoretically available to us at any time. I believe that moments of awakening or enlightenment are experienced in a very similar way – as both pure openness to spirit and total groundedness in the present moment.

Since we've already talked quite a bit about practices that help you open more to spirit, let's take a look at some ways to get you grounded in your body. A good first step is to begin a practice like yoga or Tai Chi, in which body awareness and breathing are emphasized. Unlike the typical, multi-tasking gym experience – riding a stationary bike while watching TV and checking your email – the objective with these practices is to connect mind, body and spirit, bringing the attention fully into the present moment. I have to confess that I never really understood the importance of this until I began attending a yoga studio regularly last year. Since then I've become a true believer!

Other good mind/body activities include walking or bowing meditation, singing and chanting, moving to music that inspires you or playing an instrument (sound vibration can be a great healing and grounding modality in itself). Even engaging in certain sports can become a conscious part of your spiritual practice, if you approach them with that intention. My brother is a white water kayaker, and the way he describes his time on the water – wide open, totally in the moment, full of joy – sounds a lot like a peak spiritual experience.

Allow yourself to revel in this physical existence. To be truly whole we need to *embody* the spirit, not cut one part off from the other, or value one and ignore the other. When you're open without being grounded, it's very common for your energy to be unbalanced and your moods to swing from one extreme to another. You might also find it hard to put the wonderful insights you have into actual practice in your life. The poet Kabir wrote, "Be strong then, and enter your own body; there you have a solid place for your feet." Try bringing your spiritual practice down out of the ether and putting some legs on it. Take it from one who has spent most of her life living in her head: This is a game-changer.

If you are one of the many who experienced physical or emotional trauma as a child, it's quite possible that you walk around in a dissociated state virtually all the time, numb to your body and emotions. What was a protective mechanism as a child becomes a way of life as an adult. You can't run away from the past, because those experiences remain locked in your muscles and viscera until you find a way to safely release them. As the beautifully named book by psychiatrist Bessel van der Kolk states, "The body keeps the score."

Complex PTSD is best explored with a good therapist, but literally *everyone* has stored painful emotions and experiences in their bodies (this is a large part of the Shadow Self we keep such a tight lid on). You don't have to be a victim of physical violence to have past trauma stored in your body – we all do. Just being aware of this will help you to acknowledge and process that old pain, so that it can move through and out of your energy field. All it really takes is the intention to heal, and the willingness to feel and release those uncomfortable emotions and sensations that you once fled or suppressed.

You won't have to hunt them down, either – once you start intentionally opening up to your body, you'll find that they present themselves automatically for healing (oh boy). It's like opening the door of an over-stuffed closet you've conveniently ignored for several decades. Be brave and resist the urge to shut back down when that happens.

Physically acting out can really help to release the old, stuck energy. Find some privacy so you can yell or scream or wail into a pillow. Punch the couch. Take big, deep breaths. Stand in one place and just shake your body. You can also look for therapeutic practices that work specifically on energy release, such as TRE (Trauma Releasing Exercises), Heart-Centered Hypnotherapy, and even acupuncture. Piece by piece you'll clear the stagnant energy from your body, and the more you do this, the freer and clearer both your body and spirit will feel. It's worth it, too. The false comfort of numbness is no substitute for a strong, clear energy field.

The adventure of reclaiming the energetic body as a container for the growing spirit is an ongoing one. Just as they say that we only use a small portion of our brains, I'm convinced that we only understand a small part of the power and capabilities of the mind/body/spirit when they work together under the direction of soul. Spirit and bodywork can be far more than simply healing wounds from the past, although that in itself is incredibly powerful. Beyond that, we have the capacity to continue growing and reaching for higher levels of consciousness and more purposeful use of our energy throughout our whole lives.

Holding that intention, and embracing a spirit of adventure, who knows what we can become?

I did not wish to live what was not life... I wanted to live deep and suck out all the marrow of life.
~ Henry David Thoreau

Life was meant to be lived, and curiosity must be kept alive. One must never, for whatever reason, turn his back on life.
~ Eleanor Roosevelt

An adventure is only an inconvenience rightly considered. An inconvenience is only an adventure wrongly considered.
~ G.K. Chesterton

CHAPTER FIVE
Dark Times

If a man wishes to be sure of the road he treads on, he must close his eyes and walk in the dark.
~ St. John of the Cross

At last we come to the chapter that was the reason I began writing another book in the first place. A few years ago, I was going through a very dark period after my long-time marriage fell apart and I had to leave a beloved home for good. I felt incredibly isolated every time I saw the happy lives portrayed by friends and acquaintances on Facebook. I was sad and angry and scared, yes, but far more painful was the feeling that I was somehow also *wrong* for not being "okay."

Some of the pressure to be happy came from outside – it's difficult to watch a loved one suffer, and we understandably want to see them feeling good again, ASAP. (I get that, Mom.) But much of it also came from myself. I kept thinking that I *should* be able to just "get over this," find the lesson in it, wrap it up nicely and ride off into a rosy sunset. When that didn't happen – when I simply kept on feeling sad and angry and scared much of the time, in spite of my therapy and meditating and affirmations and journaling – the feeling of deep inadequacy grew, and along with it a paralyzing sense of isolation and loneliness. What was wrong with me, anyway?

I believe that the self-help industry and many aspects of the contemporary spiritual movement suffer from a massive case of spiritual bypass. We as a society in general are unwilling to feel our uncomfortable feelings, and deeply discouraging of those who are either unable or unwilling to put on a "brave face" for public consumption (if not private!). Even when painful feelings aren't condemned outright, they are seen as something necessary but deplorable, to be gotten over as quickly as possible. We use wonderful practices like meditation not to truly be present to our experience, but instead as a way to leapfrog over the nasty bits in an effort to reclaim our lovely, peaceful "Zen" attitude.

I'm calling bull on this. I want to reclaim the right to feel bad without apology. No, it's much bigger than that: I want to establish the *necessity* to feel bad in order to grow your soul. When we rush through dark times, we relinquish some of the greatest opportunities we will ever be given to grow into our spiritual potential. When we deny ourselves the full expression of our humanity, we become lesser humans. When we attempt to barricade ourselves against life's difficulties, we deprive ourselves of the full experience of life. None of that is justified by the avoidance of a little – or even a lot – of pain.

Dark times are non-negotiable. You *will* have them; the only question is whether you will run from them (and keep on running, because ultimately there's no getting away) or let them have their way with you, willingly. If you walk through them, they will change you for the better. If you run, you may be running from your greatest gift. If you fight, it's a losing battle. You will only exhaust yourself, without ever killing the demon. If you simply put your head in the demon's mouth, as in the old Buddhist story, it becomes a friend. There it is again: Paradox, the soul of Soul.

Since metaphors make this, the most difficult subject of all, easier to grasp on an instinctive, visceral level, I'll be using them liberally in this chapter. We understand in our bones that rain is necessary to make a garden grow, even when we wish it could always be sunny. We get that when you're in the middle of a long, dark tunnel you must keep moving in order to reach the light. We see and recognize the literal landscape of the heart and can use the healing power of metaphor to guide us back to wholeness – not diminished, but stronger and wider and deeper and higher for our journeys in the wasteland.

Desert places

When I was first wandering in my own desert place, my greatest desire was to find a way out as quickly as possible. I didn't *want* a desert – I wanted a lush valley, full of greenery and life and running water. I didn't have eyes at first to take in the subtle beauty of the desert. The seemingly barren earth was inhospitable; the creatures were mysterious and elusive. I wanted out. If I had had my way, I never would have learned to love the desert places in my life. I didn't have a choice, it seems. As determinedly as I looked for the way out, it evaded me. And so I kept on wandering, and eventually found that even the desert is hospitable to the soul.

Many saints and prophets have found the same thing. The forty-days-and-forty-nights theme of trials in the desert is long and illustrious. Modern day saints have similar stories. The one that strikes me most is Nelson Mandela's twenty-seven years of imprisonment. He couldn't have known that that barren, seemingly endless and pointless exile was preparing him to play an epic role as peacemaker for an entire nation. Would he have had the moral strength to do what he did without those years of patient endurance? It's hard to imagine. Holocaust survivor Viktor Frankl wrote, "When we are no longer able to change a situation, we are challenged to change ourselves."

This is what happens when you stay in the desert long enough: It changes you. Mostly it changes the way you see. Surrounded by good fortune and plenty, your senses grow dull. In the desert, you come to notice and feel deep gratitude for every small beauty and helpful thing. You pare down inside as well; pull inward as desert things do. This is where real life begins to grow again, deep inside. Maybe that's why desert times are so conducive to soul growth. Ego is lush and verdant, but superficial and short-lived. Soul's growth is less obvious, but deep-rooted and lasting. It's not visible to the world, and often not even to ourselves, for a very long time. The world (and ego) will go for quick, showy gains any time over the long, painstaking work of cultivating deep roots.

Ego, of course, is behind the desperate desire to be out of the desert and into the lush valley. It has an image to protect, and wandering alone in the desert is *not* cool. (A good many of those photos on Facebook are posted by ego.) At most, our Social Selves might obliquely refer to a "rough patch" and then laugh it off or change the subject. When I was struggling, even with my closest friends – even with my *therapist,* for God's sake – I would try to put a positive spin on it. There is so much shame in not having your act together, maybe even more so when you're a person who consciously strives to be "spiritual."

This is pride versus humility again. It's the deep unwillingness to admit that we don't have it all together, all the time. The unwillingness to be seen as hurting, as confused, as – God forbid – actually *needing* help rather than giving it. This humbling in the eyes of the world (even if it's only our perception) is what makes ego squirm the most. Which is yet another reason we should embrace the dark times. Have you noticed that people who have never been humbled are usually not people you want to be around? When it all comes easily, when everyone loves you and success follows you around like a devoted pet dog, ego takes the credit and becomes unbearable. As hard as it is to have that bubble of pride burst, it's actually more like lancing an infected boil – painful but necessary. It will make you much stronger and healthier in the end.

John Adams, our second President, knew a lot about public humiliation. He was a tireless advocate of independence and democracy, but widely disliked and misunderstood, especially in comparison to his popular friend and rival, Thomas Jefferson. He wrote, "… upon the stage of life, while conscience claps, let the world hiss!

On the contrary if conscience disapproves, the loudest applauses of the world are of little value." For conscience read soul, and for the world, ego. These two forces will always be at odds, as they have opposing agendas (love versus fear, remember). Adams's wife, Abigail, a hero in her own right, encouraged him: "It is not in the still calm of life… that great characters are formed. The habits of a vigorous mind are formed in contending with difficulties. Great necessities call out great virtues."

When you're sitting in the mud of some humiliation or struggle or defeat or disappointment, it's difficult to imagine that great gifts are right there with you in the mud. One writer who helped me to understand this was Pema Chödrön. I've read almost every book she's written, and the gist of them is this: Experience what you are experiencing fully. Stay there in the mud and feel around instead of spending all your energy trying to get out. You might be surprised by what you find.

Sit in the mud

Yes, this is the same theme, different metaphor. I hope I'm making my point! Take a mud bath, and take it lying down. Feel the quality of the mud; in other words, really feel your feelings, experience this part of life as fully as you experience the good times. They are two sides of the same coin. You won't be here forever, any more than you'll be walking on Easy Street forever. It only feels like forever when you're clawing desperately for purchase. All that wild energy spent resisting only pulls you down further, like quicksand.

But remember, this attitude of acceptance refers to your *internal* experience. You should continue to take whatever steps are appropriate to your external circumstances. We won't have that whole conversation again, but I just wanted to pop in that little reminder, because it's so easy to hear the words "Don't resist" and think that it's the same as "Be passive." Not at all. Don't resist your internal experience. Go ahead and resist the external like hell if you need to.

So there you are, not resisting, sitting in the mud. What happens now? Well, not much. As Sue Monk Kidd writes, "… in many ways waiting is the missing link in the transformation process. I'm not referring to waiting as we're accustomed to it, but waiting as the passionate and contemplative crucible in which new life and spiritual wholeness can be birthed." This is where *being* comes in, and intention. This part takes patience and faith.

The gifts will find you, but they don't usually show up with a whole lot of fanfare. They steal in quietly, and then one day when you're in the midst of everyday life you suddenly find that you have this great well of compassion in you. Or maybe it's a quiet little song of gratitude. Or you get an idea that sets your life off in a completely different direction. There's no telling what the gifts will be, or when they'll show up, but it's *guaranteed* to happen. (You'll have to trust me on that.) Soul growth is absolutely quiet and still and hidden until, all of a sudden, it's not. If you want to grow a massive oak tree you're not going to do it with the root system of a tumbleweed. Deep roots take time, and they grow where you can't see them or impatiently track their progress.

I like this quote by Kahlil Gibran: "The deeper that sorrow carves into your being, the more joy you can contain." I think it's true that the capacity for great feeling has to go both ways. If you're only willing to feel a thimbleful of sadness, then that's all the joy you can hold as well. And even the emotions that we think of as wholly negative, like anger or fear, only truly become negative when they're denied the opportunity to be seen and heard. This denial of the more painful emotions is at the heart of our unwillingness to experience dark times, so let's look more closely at the many strategies we use to avoid having to experience them.

These strategies are both internal and external, and can be generally classified as either suppression or reaction. **Suppression** comes in three flavors. *Numbing* can be external (alcohol, drugs) and/or internal (denial, dissociation). *Distraction* is most often external (shopping, TV, simply keeping too busy to feel), but I think of spiritual bypass as a form of internal distraction (I'm too busy being happy to feel sad or mad!). With both numbing and distraction, it's likely there is very little conscious awareness that negative emotions are behind the behaviors. The third form of internal suppression, which I call *stuffing,* is more overt and conscious. You know that you're angry or sad or scared, but you feel so much shame or contempt for yourself for having those feelings that you simply cut them off at the knees. It's the Godfather approach to suppressing emotions.

Reaction has two forms. *Obsessing* will generally be both internal and external, as you constantly ruminate on the emotions and the stories behind them, telling them over and over to yourself and to anyone else who will listen. It's like constantly poking your finger into an open wound to make sure it's still there. *Acting out* can take obviously external forms (explosions of anger, hand-wringing drama, and so on), but it also comes in internal or self-directed varieties (cutting and other forms of self-harm).

As you can see, there's a wide repertoire of strategies available at a moment's notice to help you avoid dealing with those uncomfortable feelings. You might quibble with me that, with acting out at least, you *are* experiencing your negative feelings. Isn't expressing them freely what we're supposed to do? I actually used to believe this myself. I grew up in a family that actively advocated suppression of uncomfortable emotions. I saw my mother cry *once*. I witnessed *one* episode of briefly raised voices between my parents. In my entire childhood. This is heavy-duty suppression, folks. So my reaction to this was to become a person who freely expressed my anger, sadness and fear, all over anyone who had the misfortune to be standing in my vicinity. It was not pretty.

So, no, reaction isn't a skillful way to process uncomfortable emotions. As Stephen Levine wrote about anger, "... no matter how much we have emoted this feeling, we have never felt rid of it for long. We become exhausted before we can get it all out. The involuntary emoting of anger just creates more of the same." Yes, I can personally vouch for that. And suppression just keeps the emotions stuck in your body, as we discussed in the previous chapter. So what *does* work to skillfully process those uncomfortable emotions?

The first thing is to realize that they're only uncomfortable to your ego. Soul isn't uncomfortable with anger, sadness and fear, because soul knows that you're *always* safe and well, no matter what state your emotions are in. When you get into that mindset, a lot of the drama these emotions generate drops away. Then you just bring your attention to them, name them if you want (but don't get caught up in words or stories), and let them be. Just hold the space open for them to move through your body at their own pace. Have a cup of tea, take a walk, treat yourself like you're a fragile object made of glass for a little bit (you aren't, but that will soothe your poor ego, and ego is really just trying in its own fearful way to keep you safe, after all).

Ego puts all of these conditions on life because it really doesn't believe that you'll be okay otherwise. Ego is so very brittle and fragile, it wants to protect itself from even the littlest bumps that come along, and the big bumps send it into pure panic mode. Soul, being eternal, is resilient in a way ego can never be. Soul is like a honey badger – nothing scares it. The well-being at the core of soul is what makes it possible to aim for that highest of all spiritual paths, which is *unconditional joy*.

Unconditional joy

Many people use the term "unconditional happiness," but I make a distinction between joy and happiness. To me, happiness is automatically conditional and temporary, based on having good or pleasant things happen to you. Joy is a much more subtle and resilient feeling of underlying well-being that can co-exist with unpleasant circumstances and uncomfortable emotions (which is what keeps it from being another form of spiritual bypass).

Thus, it can truly be unconditional and eternal. This is the path Michael Singer – he of *The Surrender Experiment* – was taking when he chose to give up his attachment to having his "personal preferences" met.

It's not that it's bad to know what you like and to enjoy it when you get it. This is not Puritanism in any way, shape or form. Personal preferences are great as long as you don't insist on having them met in order to feel good. Don't let your sense of well-being and joy be conditional on them. And the secret to doing that is: *Dismantle the ego,* since it's the fragile ego that insists on having its conditions met in order to be happy. The soul feels joy no matter what's going on in the world around it.

Here's a metaphor that helps me visualize both the problem and its solution. Imagine that soul is a river of joy flowing through you. The incidents that occur during a day are like logs and sticks floating in the current. As long as the channel is free and clear, they can float along happily without disturbing much of anything. But if there's even a little obstruction in the stream – an attachment to having a preference met – some of the "sticks" will inevitably bump up against it. This is what happens, many times a day, when your conditions for being happy aren't met. You feel a little jolt of anger or fear or impatience (or whatever) when some circumstance or incident bumps up against your ideas of how life should be.

The jolt itself, although unpleasant, isn't really the problem. The problem is how we deal with it. Instead of going straight to the obstruction – the attachment – and releasing it, so that the joy can flow unimpeded, we mostly just keep trying harder and harder to stop anything from bumping up against our preferences. We try to control the circumstances of our lives so that nothing upsets our little (and growing bigger) pile of sticks and logs, but our ability to do that is very limited. Pretty soon all kinds of flotsam and jetsam are getting hung up there, and over time the little logjam turns into a huge pile that juts out into the river, cutting it down to a trickle.

This structure is your ego, getting bumped and jostled by every little thing floating down the river. No wonder we try to reinforce and protect it, but the bigger we build it, the less joy gets through. What we think is protecting us from pain is actually the very thing cutting us off from our joy. Here's a different idea: Why not use the logs floating down the river – all those big and little things that bump up against the ego structure – to actually break up the logjam and dismantle it, instead of making it bigger? Rather than bracing against those jolts and resisting them, what if we saw each one as an opportunity to let just a little bit more ego and attachment go floating off downstream?

Yes, those "hits" are uncomfortable, but every bit of the structure we let go also lets a little more joy flow through. Every attachment and condition we release is one less place for the circumstances of life to bump up against. The circumstances themselves aren't the real problem. Let's face it – there will always be something your ego doesn't like! Since we have no way to stop the logs from coming down the river, the only effective choice is to let them pass on by without internally resisting them. There's real exhilaration in the process of freeing yourself, and the reward is the renewed flow of joy that, once released from obstructions, simply carries the logs downstream. When you get hooked on the process of dismantling your ego (and you will) the "hits" you experience, while still not pleasant, can simply be accepted as signs that there's something else you need to let go.

Tending the flow of unconditional joy like this is a spiritual path in itself, and the work of a lifetime. As Michael Singer put it, "It seemed that the more challenges life put me through, the less my inner energy flow was affected by outer conditions. What years of willful meditation had not gotten rid of, life's situations and challenges were rooting out of me. As long as I made getting rid of myself [the ego] my only goal, every situation was a fruitful experience."

Alchemy
Once again, the things we flee and resist turn out to be our greatest gifts. The demon is really our friend in disguise. Like Rumpelstiltskin in the classic fairy tale, we find that the soul is capable of spinning dross into gold. This is where real magic comes in: That we have no way of knowing what our troubles really mean or their true place in the unfolding of our lives' purpose. We just have to keep walking through the tunnel, walking in the dark, trusting that somewhere up ahead the light is waiting.

In the poem *Letters of Fire* Kahlil Gibran writes:

> Yonder in the hereafter
> We shall see the beating of our hearts
> And comprehend the meaning of
> our godlike state,
> That in this day we hold as naught
> Because despair is ever at our heels.
>
> The crying that today we call a weakness
> Shall appear on the morrow
> A link in man's existence.
> The fret and toil that requite us not
> Shall abide with us to tell our glory.
> The afflictions that we bear
> Shall be to us a crown of honor.

I fervently hope and believe that most of the heartaches and difficulties we endure in this life will become clear with time. Some things we might never really understand in this lifetime, which is part of the mystery. It's utterly human and understandable to wish to avoid pain. To be "happy" is usually our greatest wish, for ourselves and our loved ones, but the truth is that this wish runs counter to our highest good and ultimate joy.

Let's all pause for a giant sigh of resignation here, because this is not easy to accept.

Psychiatrist Scott Peck wrote: "Once we truly know that life is difficult – once we truly understand and accept it – then life is no longer difficult. Because once it is accepted, the fact that life is difficult no longer matters." This, then, is the ultimate difference between ego and soul. To ego, life is *all about* trying to avoid difficulty. It's about attachment to pleasure and aversion to pain. It's about protecting the self at all costs. It's about fear.

The soul is never afraid. To the soul, difficulty and joy (and everything else) are ultimately the same substance, indistinguishable: Dross and gold, demon and friend, most dire calamity and greatest gift. It's all love in disguise, every bit of it.

It is difficulties that show what men are.
~ Epictetus

Affliction is a good man's shining time.
~ Edward Young

God judged it better to bring good out of evil than to suffer no evil at all.

~ St. Augustine

CONCLUSION
The Meaning of Life

To do the useful thing, to say the courageous thing, to contemplate the beautiful thing: that is enough for one man's life.
~ T.S. Eliot

Okay, hopefully I'm not over-promising here… the meaning of life is a big subject to take on in a few concluding pages. But no matter how high-flown my prose gets, let me keep this discussion grounded by saying that the actual process of living a meaningful life doesn't get much more complicated than this: Do the useful thing, say the courageous thing, contemplate the beautiful thing.

Everything I've written in this book leads back to this: Embody your soul. See past the narrow confines of the ego's point of view. There's so much more to life, and so much more to being human, than the ego's little agenda can cover. To employ one more metaphor, I like to think of life as being like one of those Balinese shadow theaters, where the audience only sees the shadows that the puppets throw on a curtain. The real life is going on at a deeper level we can't see with our physical eyes.

And you can extend the metaphor even further by considering that our souls are like the puppet masters, knowing exactly what is going on all the time, walking us through the stories of our lives with clear intent and purpose, no matter how chaotic and random the storyline might seem to us. We simply don't have all of the information, which is obviously the way we set up this time/space experiment to be. Ego, the Social Self, takes what information we have and desperately tries to make sense of the world. We can believe what ego tells us, or simply recognize that there's a much bigger game afoot, on a much broader stage, and cooperate to the best of our abilities with it.

Ego isn't trying to trick us on purpose; it's just a child who believes the dream is real, while soul is the parent who knows that there's really nothing to fear. It helps to see ego as this frightened child in need of soothing, rather than an enemy to battle. When you feel the fear stirring, even if it's masquerading as anger or judgment or impatience, send it some love. Treat your ego with compassion – but think carefully before putting that frightened child in charge of your life!

Overcoming illusion (ego) and embodying the soul is my personal mission, and also the meaning of the spiritual name I was given. "Maya" is the Sanskrit word for illusion, so "A-maya" means "without illusion." When soul is in charge, the illusion of ego loses its power over us. We literally wake up from the dream and see for the first time with clarity, looking at everything and everyone through the eyes of love, rather than the eyes of fear.

If that sounds like a miracle to you, you're right. And it's not the only one you'll find along the path of soul growth:

1. You will feel a deep peace. This happens when you stop resisting life and your own emotions. You find that you can "contain multitudes" (in the words of Walt Whitman) without losing your center. You stop reacting and start responding, consciously, to the people and events of your life.

2. You will stop faking it, in any way. The more you know and trust your Authentic Self, the less you will be able to tolerate the illusions of the Social Self. You will come to recognize the voice of ego instantly in yourself and in others, and automatically question it. The inner guidance system that steers you unerringly to your highest good will be up and running.

3. Everything will change, even if nothing changes. Even though externally it seems that not much has changed in my life since my divorce, on the inside everything has changed. The same set of circumstances that had me feeling hopeless and depressed twelve months ago now feel joyful and exciting. I'm so grateful for this, because I know that my joy isn't based on something that happened *to* me, but something that happened *in* me.

4. Everyone around you will change too. Once you start consciously choosing soul, the effects will ripple out to the people around you as well. William Butler Yeats described what happens beautifully: "We can make our minds so like still water that beings gather about us, that they may see their own images, and so live for a moment with a clearer, perhaps even with a fiercer, life because of our quiet."

For a moment... but that's all it takes. If you give soul even half a chance it will grow and flourish. Your Authentic Self, who you really are, is incredibly resilient. Venture past the fragile Social Self, swim the stormy seas of the Shadow Self, and you'll find the place of unconditional love and joy at the center of your being.

It's never too late to change your vote from Ego to Soul. There's never a time when fear is too much for love to handle. Ultimately, the meaning of life is just this: Love. Love yourself and love others. Love the hard times as well as the good. Love your body. Love your ego. Love the earth. *Love.*

One should always be on the trail of one's own deepest nature. For it is the fearless living out of your own essential nature that connects you to the Divine.
~ *Henry David Thoreau*

All know that the drop merges into the ocean, but few know that the ocean merges into the drop.
~ *Kabir*

Recommended Reading

Michael Singer
The Surrender Experiment
The Untethered Soul

Lynne Twist
The Soul of Money

Pema Chödrön
The Places That Scare You
(and anything else)

Diane Zimberoff
Breaking Free from the Victim Trap

Martha Beck
Expecting Adam
(this might be my favorite soul book of all time)

David Schnarch:
Passionate Marriage

Stephen Cope
The Great Work of Your Life

M. Scott Peck
The Road Less Traveled (an oldie but goodie)

Tara Brach
Radical Acceptance

Liz Gilbert
Big Magic (on creativity)

Cheryl Strayed
Tiny Beautiful Things

Xorin Balbes
Soul Space
(arranging your home to support your soul's expression)

Carol S. Pearson
The Hero Within

ABOUT THE AUTHOR

Amaya Pryce is a spiritual coach and writer living in the Pacific Northwest. For coaching or speaking inquiries, or to follow her blog, please visit www.amayapryce.com.

Made in the USA
San Bernardino, CA
25 January 2020

63601973R00085